PLAYING
THE
BEAUTIFUL
GAME

JAG SHOKER

PLAYING
THE
BEAUTIFUL
GAME

*Inspirational thoughts to help you
play well, work well and live well*

First published in 2011 by
Infinite Ideas Limited
36 St Giles
Oxford
OX1 3LD
United Kingdom
www.infideas.com

A CIP catalogue record for this book is available from the British Library

ISBN 978–1–906821–94–4

Text designed and typeset by Cylinder
Printed and bound in Great Britain by
CPI Antony Rowe, Chippenham and Eastbourne

CONTENTS

ACKNOWLEDGEMENTS

I'd like to dedicate this book to all those wonderful people who have supported, challenged and inspired me throughout my life, especially my parents and family.

Specifically in relation to the writing of this book I'd like to thank:

My wife, Harj, for believing in both me and the idea behind this book;

My dear friend Tirath for the clarity and honesty of the feedback he provided on the verses;

My dear friend Marie for kindly pointing me in the right direction all those years ago when I first thought of writing a book;

My dear friend Yiannis for inspiring me to write a book that may be of benefit and value to those who read it.

Finally I'd like to thank the team at Infinite Ideas, the publisher of this book, for the enthusiasm and willingness they have shown in making this book a reality.

INTRODUCTION

Life, sport and business are all, at times, games. There are goals we'd like to achieve and there are challenges we must face. There are successes we hope to enjoy and there are disappointments from which we must grow.

Your success within a game depends so much upon the clarity, strength and purpose with which you play the game. Within this book, I have written a series of verses that I hope will inspire you to play your best game wherever you're hoping for success.

Each verse is based upon three central ideas:

- The pitch represents the stage upon which you grow, strive and seek to succeed.
- The game is whatever you imagine it to be. It could be the sport you play, the business you're involved in or the life you lead.
- The beautiful game symbolises your most inspired performance; one that draws the best from you and from those around you.

Through each verse I have expressed what I have learned so far through my own personal journey and the insights I have been privileged to gain through coaching and assisting others to achieve greater success in their professional and personal lives.

The verses themselves express different qualities, such as awareness, intention, integrity, inner strength, expansion, balance, harmony, leadership and inspired movement, that will inspire you to play your game beautifully.

It is my hope that the verses will help you to refine each quality and bring you greater success and fulfilment. You may find that working on one quality has a positive effect on other areas of your life and also on those around you. For when any game is played beautifully there is the perfect coming together of all things.

Jag Shoker

July 2011

AWARENESS

*Develop a greater awareness of the game and of the
opportunities and challenges inherent within it.
Recognise the greater potential within you
to do more and be more.*

1.

All of life is played out before you.

The beautiful game has much to reveal

To those who look.

Your approach to life

Determines the way you play.

How you compete on its stage

Reveals much about who you are.

2.

All movement emanates from hidden depths.

Every twist and turn gives cause for reflection.

Look deeper into the play

And the meaning concealed within it.

With greater understanding

Strive to know the beautiful game.

3.

Study the game,

To gain knowledge of it.

Experience the game,

To gain wisdom from it.

4.

Seek your inspiration.

Let it lift your game.

The more inspired you are

The more beauty you create.

5.

Recognise the potential within you.

See how far with it you can go.

Be humble if it takes you a great way.

From wherever you believe it flows,

Acknowledge the source.

6.

Know what stands in your way.

Know what impacts your performance.

Know what holds back your potential.

Know your limitations

In order to transcend them.

7.

A hard game will be a true test of character.

When the pressure is on

Your inner workings stand revealed.

When your character is laid bare on the pitch,

Learn what the game has to teach you.

8.

There is the vision you develop on the pitch.

There is the perspective you gain off it.

Use your time on the sidelines to reflect.

Think what more you can bring.

Resolve to come back stronger.

9.

When you witness a miracle on the pitch,

Know that a process brought it forth.

What is achieved once,

Can be achieved again.

10.

The game is ever changing.

Do not get lost in the movement.

Focus each moment on what is important.

Refocus regularly should you forget.

11.

Play with appreciation.

Appreciation cultivates awareness.

Awareness creates depth.

From such depths

Unleash greater potential.

12.

Appreciate your body and what moves you.

Appreciate your mind and what guides you.

Appreciate your will and what drives you.

Appreciate all that is good,

That comes through you.

13.

Appreciate the team that supports you.

Appreciate the opponent that tests you.

Appreciate the crowd that inspires you.

Appreciate all the game gives to you.

INTENTION

*Know your true motive for playing the
game and what it is that you're seeking to achieve.
Strive to play the game with purpose and passion.*

14.

Know why you play the game.

Know who you are playing for.

Be clear about what drives you.

Know how far your motivation will take you.

15.

Play for riches

And emptiness may consume you.

Play for glory

And success may elude you.

Play for fame

And it may imprison you.

Play just to win

And defeat may hamper you.

Play for the pure joy of the game

And it will fulfil you.

16.

Play with purpose

And opportunities will be drawn to you.

Play with presence

And the way will open up for you.

Play with passion

And you will blaze the path before you.

17.

What you imagine in your mind,

You can create on the pitch.

See the game before you play the game.

Visualise success.

18.

Use the mind positively.

Learn from games gone by.

Live fully the game you're playing.

Imagine the best for games to come.

19.

Your thoughts about the game,

Influence your feelings towards it.

If you don't feel right about the game,

Change your thoughts towards it.

20.

Start as you mean to go on.

Intend to make your mark.

Move with true purpose.

When there is everything to play for

Your intention is everything.

21.

When desire is strong,

And your commitment is unwavering,

Passion sparks the game into life.

22.

Don't wait for the crowd to inspire you,

Inspire the crowd.

Win them over with your passion.

Impress them with your effort.

Delight them with your skill.

Reward them for their support.

23.

Before you make your move

Ensure you have a firm intention.

See what you want to do.

Know you have the power

To make it happen.

The stronger the intention

The greater the success.

24.

Much can be deciphered

From how you take your opportunity.

If you are aware

You set yourself right.

If you have passion

You move with purpose.

If you have belief

You follow through with conviction.

INTEGRITY

Be responsible for the game you play
and the effect it has on others.
Seek to win in the right way and
through the right means.

25.

The game can confer greatness upon you.

When you reach the heights,

Know others will look up to you.

When leading the way,

Be responsible for those who follow you.

26.

The game can confer riches upon you.

When wealth flows from it,

Continue to invest back into it.

There is always more to gain.

There is always more to give.

27.

Play to win the game.

But also to win

The trust of your team,

The support of the crowd,

The respect of the opposition.

Win these and even in defeat

Much has been gained.

28.

If defeated by a worthy opponent,

Learn from the game.

If defeated by a fortunate opponent,

Stay poised.

Good fortune has a tendency to balance out.

Hard work however will always reap its reward.

29.

Fail to bring others into the game

And you may frustrate the play.

Try to do it alone

And you may unbalance your team.

Ignore the movement of others

And you may waste your resources.

Play your own game

But be accountable for what you do.

30.

Always play fair.

Do not seek advantage through dishonest means.

The only person you cheat is yourself,

Of the opportunity to cultivate your skill,

And of the joy of overcoming a challenge.

31.

If you suffer injustice on the pitch,

Do not lose sight of what is fair.

Stay within the bounds of the game.

Have faith the wrongs will be put right.

32.

Within the game

You can deceive others,

You cannot deceive yourself.

Actions seen or unseen,

Thoughts expressed or unexpressed,

Remain with you.

Know their effects will go before you.

33.

Consider your next move.

Does it help or hinder your team?

Build or destroy the play?

Add or take away from the game?

Be responsible now for what you do next.

34.

Be accountable on the pitch.

Take ownership over how you play.

Don't blame others when things go wrong.

Preserve your power to put things right.

INNER STRENGTH

Use the power within you to meet the challenges you face.

Respond with strength when the game tests you.

See all challenges as opportunities for you to

grow and unleash greater potential.

35.

The further you go
The more the game reveals.
With greater perseverance
More is endured,
More is experienced,
More is learned.

36.

If the game unfolds in undesirable ways,

Know self-pity will only hold you back.

Work now on what is in your gift.

You have the capacity within,

To meet the challenge without.

37.

There is the game played on the pitch.

There is the game played in the mind.

Positive and negative voices compete for attention.

The voice you listen to grows in power.

38.

Embrace a challenge on the pitch.

For it is an opportunity

To test your mettle,

To build more strength,

To learn more about yourself,

To unleash greater potential.

39.

Make failure your ally in the game.

Let it point to a better way.

Work on what it is beneficial to change.

Take heart from what already works.

40.

When challenged hard,

Be strong in your response.

Call upon your strength

And it will grow.

Let weakness set in

And it will take over.

41.

When your game is plagued by doubt,

Rely upon the greater power within.

Recall its brilliance in the past.

See it inspire the game ahead.

42.

When others criticise your game,

Ask yourself,

Is there truth in what has been said?

If no,

Have the courage to play your game.

If so,

Have the courage to change your game.

43.

Build your defence on inner strength.

Develop your power,

To stand firm,

To stand together,

To withstand any challenge.

44.

Through a strong body flows greater energy,

Through a strong heart greater courage,

Through a strong mind greater will.

When all three align

You bring greater power

Into your game.

45.

With the odds stacked against you,

And the game slipping away,

Know if hope still glimmers,

The game is still alive.

Fortunes can change in an instant.

46.

When the eyes of the world are on you,

Be comfortable with its expectant gaze.

See yourself what needs to be done.

Focus your energies to make it happen.

EXPANSION

Sense the greater possibilities in the game.
Play courageously in the moment and expand
your ability to do more and be more.

47.

Let courage win over fear.

Let creativity win over convention.

Let beauty win over ugliness.

Be free in your movement.

Beauty lies in expression not repression.

48.

Be in the moment.

Let the game flow from there.

Add spontaneity to what is tried and tested.

Transcend what is known.

Create what is sublime.

49.

If your body hardens you lose flexibility.

If your mind hardens you lose choice.

Move through choice rather than compulsion.

Value your freedom.

Open up the game.

50.

As your ability expands,

Greater trust can be placed upon it.

Allow things to happen naturally.

Your best will unfold effortlessly.

51.

The game may be fast-moving
But the mind can be still.
The crowd may be deafening
But the mind can be silent.
The space may be tight
But the mind can be open.
A mind thus inspired
Can channel brilliance.

52.

Never forget the basics.

Use them to create a rhythm.

When you do the simple things well,

The difficult things happen of their own accord.

53.

Do not be imprisoned by past performances.

Good or bad, let them go.

No matter what your level,

Know you have greater potential.

54.

Play within yourself

And you risk losing your edge.

Worry about not making mistakes

And you can play it too safe.

Try to be too perfect

And you may lose your flow.

Find your edge

And courage will take you beyond it.

55.

Do you dare to win

Or are you afraid to lose?

Do you unleash your gift

Or do you hold it back?

When the moment calls,

Your level of courage will define it.

56.

Continually hone your skill.

Forever expand your potential.

Strive always for greater strength.

Grow with every game.

57.

When you appear to have mastered,

What you know of the game,

Look closer for what can take you beyond.

Know an enhancement may be fine,

But what flows from it can be immense.

58.

Savour your ability,

To become more than you were,

And consider that thrilling thought.

What if the possibilities are indeed endless?

Why not imagine, what else?

Why not dream, what next?

BALANCE

Empower your game in a sustainable way.
Realise there is a time to push forward and a time
to hold back, a time to strive and a time to rest.
Infuse your game with greater vitality.

59.

Be balanced.

Be poised.

Be ready.

60.

The game will ebb and flow.

There are times when the momentum is with you.

And times when it is against you.

Know when to capitalise and when to consolidate.

61.

Know your rival's strengths.
But do not lose sight of your own.
In preparing to defend
Have also a plan of attack.
Always give your rival something
With which to contend.

62.

Learn to go left or right.

Be comfortable going forward or back.

Be at ease when leading

Or supporting the play.

Balance will unlock the game for you.

63.

Let go of what doesn't serve you on the pitch.

Be light.

Be free.

Be responsive.

64.

Treat all games as special.

Cherish your time on the pitch.

Play for the love of the game,

And you will always rise to the occasion.

65.

Bring elegance to the game.

Run smoothly.

Move gracefully.

Use power when needed.

Create more with less.

66.

Be grounded in what you do.

Be balanced in how you move.

Be down to earth when you play.

67.

There is reason to smile.

The body relaxes.

The mind calms.

Spirit strengthens within you.

You're ready

For whatever the game throws your way.

68.

When injury strikes,

Know it is natural to heal.

In quietness let its power work.

See yourself rejuvenate.

Revitalise your game.

69.

Breathe fully.

Breathe deeply.

Breathe smoothly.

Energise your body.

Expand your mind.

Enhance your capacity for the game.

70.

There is a time to step up.

There is a time to step back.

Balance effort with rest.

Preserve your vitality.

71.

For a better rhythm:

Eat well.

Train well.

Rest well.

Sleep well.

72.

Spend time away from the game.

Take the opportunity to renew.

Return with greater vigour.

HARMONY

In harmony combine your effort and skill

with those who play the game with you.

Bring them into play at the right time and in

the right way to create wider possibilities.

73.

Played in the right spirit the game is beautiful.

There is unity in a team.

There is fairness in competition.

There is a connection with the crowd.

There is harmony in the play.

74.

Keep the game moving.

Always make yourself available.

Create space for others

And others will create space for you.

Create opportunities for others

And great opportunity will be created for you.

75.

When the time is right
Bring others into play.
In doing so create trust
And through trust create harmony.
Great moves will flow from it.

76.

When the right thing
Happens at the right time
In the right way,
There is joy,
There is harmony,
There is perfection.

77.

Form a unit.

Move in harmony.

Play as a collective.

Together more is possible.

78.

Your first touch is the key.

It is what brings you in to the game.

With it you can create harmony

Or kill momentum.

From it all possibilities can come alive.

79.

Refine your skill.

Perfect your game.

Have more to give.

Have more to share.

80.

Know when to act.

Within the game

Timing is everything.

Be patient,

Respect the timing.

Be decisive,

Perfect the timing.

LEADERSHIP

*Seek to shape the game and direct the play
with greater awareness and understanding.
Inspire your team and expand its potential.*

81.

Be visionary in your thinking.

Be imaginative when shaping the play.

But let your ideas be tangible.

Make your instructions workable.

And your game plan achievable.

82.

Prepare well.

Perfect your plan.

But when the game kicks off let go.

Trust your players will succeed.

Allow the play to unfold.

83.

Stifle your players
And they may lose their vitality.
Grant too much freedom
And the team may lose its shape.
Balance form with fluidity.
Discipline with freedom.

84.

When called for use anger.

When necessary raise your voice.

Know also that where there is respect,

A quiet word can work wonders.

85.

Shouting instructions

Doesn't guarantee that they'll be followed.

Forcing others to do as you say

Doesn't mean that they will.

Inspire rather than coerce your players.

Win them over with your words.

86.

Talk with honesty.

Manage with integrity.

Be guided by what is right for the team.

87.

Believe in potential.

Have faith your players can grow.

Take their development to heart.

Let this shape your coaching,

So you may rightly shape their game.

88.

Let your philosophy guide your coaching.

Let your coaching guide your play.

Let how you play speak for itself.

Be content to work from behind the scenes.

89.

The movement on the pitch is visible to all.

Yet there is much hidden beneath the surface.

When looking for an explanation to the play,

Look deeper within each player for the causes.

INSPIRED MOVEMENT

Let your movements flow from a deeper sense and appreciation of how to play the beautiful game.

90.

Take action.

Make it happen.

Nothing is created without movement.

91.

There is a time.

There is a place.

When the occasion calls for it,

Express yourself.

92.

If your opponent knows where you're going,

He may get there before you.

When least expected

Change direction,

Change the pace,

Change the game.

93.

Do the unexpected

Be hard to contain.

Do not be bound by your opponent.

Find space to work your magic.

Free yourself

To put your mark on the game.

94.

Develop a turn of speed.

Be swift

When changing direction.

Be decisive

When making up your mind.

Harness your speed

But do not rush what you do.

95.

When space is tight,

And time is short,

Sharpen your skill.

Make the most of the moment.

96.

Move for each other,

To create the space,

To make the play,

To shape the game.

97.

A good opposition will be hard to prise open.

They will be skilled at closing you down.

You have to be patient

When there is no way to advance.

You may need to go backwards

To go forwards.

98.

When the gap opens,

And you have the edge,

Be quick to capitalise.

The quicker the game,

The more fleeting the chance.

99.

Anticipate the play.

Sense the timing.

Make your move.

Make it count.

100.

Widen your gaze.

See more of the game.

Create more options.

Have more moves.

Keep your opponent guessing.

101.

Celebrate goals.

Live the moment.

But do not be led astray.

Finish what your enthusiasm started.

Arrive where you intended to be.

Persevere to the end.